SEASON'S GREETINGS

Table of Contents

FEATURED AUTHOR

Chantelle Crowell

From CEO, FOUNDER

Dear Readers,

Welcome to the Fall/Winter 2024 issue of BWA Kids Lit! Magazine, a space where stories, imagination, and creativity come to life through the voices of Black children's authors. It is with great joy and excitement that we present this special edition, designed to inspire young readers and celebrate the rich diversity of Black literature for children.

As the seasons change and we approach the holiday season, there is no better time to nurture a love of reading in our children. Books have the power to spark imaginations, build character, and transport young minds to magical worlds. Our goal at BWA Kids Lit! is to amplify the voices of Black authors who write stories that reflect the unique experiences and dreams of children of color. This magazine offers a platform for these voices to be heard, ensuring that every child can see themselves represented in the pages of a book.

In this issue, we are proud to feature a dynamic collection of authors who are dedicated to enriching the literary landscape. From captivating picture books to adventurous tales of discovery, these stories are perfect for little readers and the parents who nurture their growth. We are also thrilled to shine the spotlight on our featured authors, showcasing their passion, their journey, and the impact they are making in the world of children's literature.

Our team has worked tirelessly to bring you a publication filled with heart, creativity, and resources that not only celebrate the written word but also offer guidance for parents and educators alike. From tips on how to encourage reading at home to insightful interviews with authors who share their inspiration, we've crafted a magazine that is both engaging and meaningful.

As we approach the close of another year, I encourage you to use this issue as an opportunity to introduce the joy of reading into your home or classroom. Every story featured here is a stepping stone toward a brighter future, where children of all backgrounds can explore their world through books that reflect their realities and expand their horizons.

Thank you for your continued support of BWA Kids Lit! Magazine. We are honored to be a part of your reading journey and excited to continue uplifting the voices of Black authors in children's literature. Together, we are creating a legacy of storytelling that will empower generations to come.

Paulette Henson

Editor - in- Chief

HOW TO HELP YOUR KIDS WITH HOMEWORK AND ENCOURAGE READING: A PARENT'S GUIDE

As a parent, supporting your child's education and fostering a love of reading can sometimes feel overwhelming, especially when homework piles up or when kids show less interest in reading. However, with a few helpful tips and strategies, you can turn homework time into a productive and enjoyable experience while encouraging a lifelong love for reading. Here's how:

1. Create a Homework Routine

Consistency is key when it comes to homework. Establishing a regular routine helps children know what to expect and makes it easier to manage their time.

Set a specific time: Choose a time each day for homework that works for your family's schedule. Some children prefer to complete homework right after school, while others may need a short break before starting.

Designate a homework space: Create a quiet, well-lit area for your child to work on their assignments. This space should be free of distractions, like toys or TV, to help them focus.

Use a timer for focus: For children who struggle to concentrate, using a timer can be helpful. Set it for short, focused intervals (like 15-20 minutes), followed by a short break to keep them engaged without feeling overwhelmed.

2. Break Down Big Tasks into Smaller Steps

Large homework assignments can feel intimidating to young students, so breaking them down into smaller, manageable steps can make the workload less daunting.

Create a checklist: Help your child create a list of smaller tasks to complete, such as reading one chapter, answering three questions, or solving a set of math problems. They can check off each task as they go, giving them a sense of accomplishment.

Read together as a family: Set an example by reading your own book or magazine during family reading time. Let your child see that reading is an enjoyable activity for everyone. Talk about what you're reading: Share what you're reading with your child, whether it's a novel, article, or even something from work. Ask them about their book, and discuss your books together to make reading a shared experience.

7. Be Patient and Encouraging

It's normal for kids to struggle with homework or reading from time to time. The key is to stay patient and offer encouragement.

Recognize effort: Celebrate the effort your child puts into their homework and reading, even if they don't get everything right. Positive reinforcement helps build their confidence and motivates them to keep going.

Help them build resilience: Teach your child that it's okay to make mistakes, as long as they keep trying. When they face challenges with a particular homework assignment or reading task, remind them that practice leads to improvement.

AUTHOR
TALONA COLEMAN
Leading the Community in Children's Literature

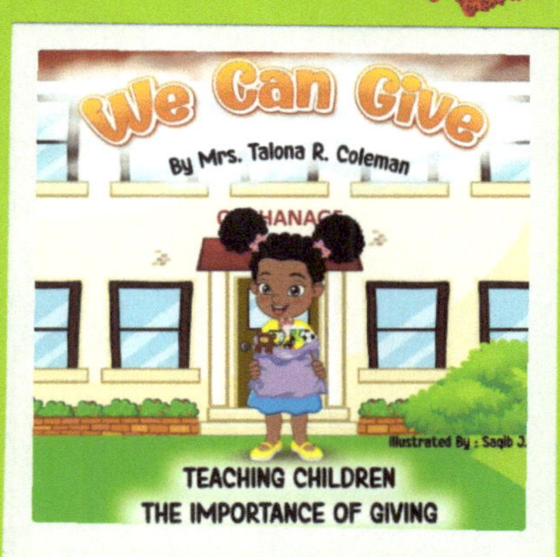

Author: Talona Coleman:

Talona Coleman is a wife, mother of 3 sons, an entrepreneur, a motivational speaker, a worshiper, Director of Heaven Sent Christian Child Care, and a children's author. She enjoys the outdoors and spending time with family and friends. She loves animals and has a dog and 2 cats. Talona is passionate about empowering children and helping them to be their best! She discovered her love for writing many years ago, as she frequently journaled her ideas and thoughts. Her 1st book "I Am Important" was released on November 10, 2022. She has since authored a host of other parent and educator approved children's books teaching valuable lessons on *acceptance, self worth, diversity, inclusion, kindness, bravery, and love!Such titles as "You Matter", "We Can Give", and "I'm Not Afraid…I'm Brave", these books were written to do "damage control" by means of changing the trajectory of what wholesome stories with morals should look like and what should be instilled in the lives of children! Talona's stories embody messages that will empower, inspire, and restore hope in the lives of each reader! Through her label Cherish Books by Talona, her mission is to teach practical lessons that motivate efficacious results!Talona's authorship journey has allowed her to collaborate with BWA Magazine (Black Women Authors), Literacy Nation Inc., BAA (Black Authors Association), Literacy Moments, Latin American Book Partners, Literacy Moments Magazine, and a host of public, private schools, child care programs, Department of Recreation, and Libraries.*

Because Talona has a heart to help children surpass academic reading levels; she has created an initiative dedicated to fostering early literacy and creative development in underserved communities. (KIDazzle ♥ Litreacy and Puppetry). **KIDazzle's mission** is to *bring joy, learning , and inspiration through interactive storytelling, literacy, and the Arts. Talona is privileged to have had the opportunity to share her writing journey, and book interviews on several platforms. Platforms such as Craft Cafe Live 2024, Bless The Author, Eloquently Speaking Broadcast Network, Welcome To The Couch, Let's Jus Talk with Kim, Garage Conversations with Char, The Author's Lounge, WWDB/AM Radio interview with Thera Martin. In addition, she has appeared in BWA (Black Women Authors) Magazine Christmas Edition 2023, and 2024 Black History edition, Pretty Women Hustle Magazine edition 2023, MetroKids June/July 2024. She also had the opportunity of her stories being read on YouTube by Fairy Tale with Heather, book signings, Reading with the Author, speaking engagements, KIDazzle puppet/literacy collaboration with Doopalpoops (Puppets with a Purpose), and roundtable discussion speaker at the 6th edition Latino Book Fair. Though grateful for all the assignments and networking opportunities she has been called too; what she most honors is her opportunity to serve others as she models a lifestyle that reflects Jesus Christ! Serving others and giving back gives her the opportunity to bestow love towards others, and for that she is forever grateful!*

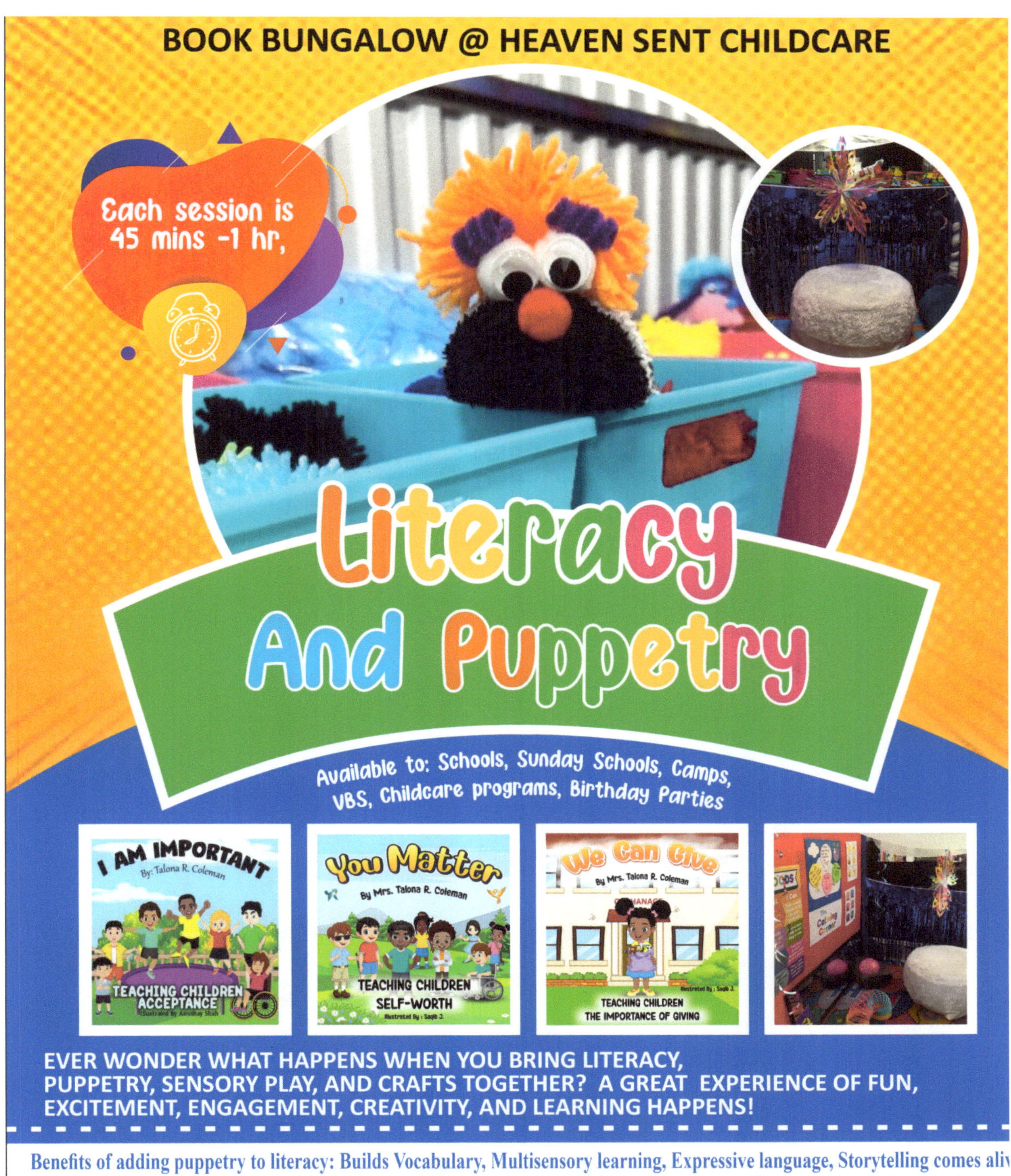

BOOK BUNGALOW @ HEAVEN SENT CHILDCARE

Each session is
45 mins -1 hr,

Literacy
And Puppetry

Available to: Schools, Sunday Schools, Camps,
VBS, Childcare programs, Birthday Parties

I AM IMPORTANT
By: Talona R. Coleman
TEACHING CHILDREN
ACCEPTANCE

You Matter
By Mrs. Talona R. Coleman
TEACHING CHILDREN
SELF-WORTH

We Can Give
By Mrs. Talona R. Coleman
TEACHING CHILDREN
THE IMPORTANCE OF GIVING

EVER WONDER WHAT HAPPENS WHEN YOU BRING LITERACY,
PUPPETRY, SENSORY PLAY, AND CRAFTS TOGETHER? A GREAT EXPERIENCE OF FUN,
EXCITEMENT, ENGAGEMENT, CREATIVITY, AND LEARNING HAPPENS!

Benefits of adding puppetry to literacy: Builds Vocabulary, Multisensory learning, Expressive language, Storytelling comes aliv

Author Talona Coleman will read 1 of her books of your choice.
Children can participate in literacy, puppetry, sensory play, or crafts.
Children will have the chance to make and take their puppets home as a special keepsake.

Onsite or offsite visits for Author Reading and puppetry.
Call for availability and rates at 215 954 7783. Rates are per person.
Time slots are between 10 am-2:30pm Monday-Friday

Kids Lit!

Sandra R. Kiser has been writing since she was a little girl. Sandra is a graduate of Wayne State University with a B.A. in English and holds a graduate certificate in Professional Writing from the University of Central Florida.

She is a Senior Proposal Manager with a construction management firm. Sandra published her first book on Alzheimer's dedicated to her mom and brother in 2020. Mysterious Wonderment: Alzheimer's Disease Becomes Your Word of the Day was #1 in Dementia, #7 in Aging Parents, and #8 in Alzheimer's on release day on Amazon. In 2022, Sandra published a children's book,

When The Amazing Adventures of the Jolly Heart Squad to help them better under stand Alzheimer's disease, along with an accompanying coloring book for younger children to introduce the main characters.

Website: alz4all.com
Instagram: sandrakiser_alz4[...]
Facebook: Sandra Kiser

The Amazing Adventures of the
Jolly Heart Squad

Alfresando befriends an elephant named Ears and a frog named Ribbitable as she takes readers on an adventure with her new friends. During their journey, they learn valuable lessons about friendships, loving and helping others, and being persistent when facing tough decisions. She discovers that her Uncle Emory may have developed early-onset Alzheimer's. It makes her sad, but she is also curious and wants to learn about the disease. Along with her best friends, the three of them begin their discovery to become smarter about Alzheimer's.

Ribbitable, the town know-it-all, knows someone who can help. When the friends travel to the tiny Village of Chedderville they meet a retired brain surgeon, Dr. Theodore McMice, who explains to them how the brain works, and how Alzheimer's begins. They also encounter the Magical Mice of Chedderville upon arrival. In the end, they learn how the disease causes adults, young and old, to lose their memory, and their ability to function on their own.

Connect with the author on Social Media
Facebook | https://www.facebook.com/sandrarkiser or Instagram | @sareki19_Sandra_Kiser

DENISE W. THARPE

Authentic Self-Published Author

Denise W. Tharpe is a five time author and storyteller. She was born in Gary Indiana. She has been an educator for over 20 years, which is what encouraged her to become an Author. Denise has a Bachelors of Art degree in Business Administration from Strayer University. She has been married to her husband Vincent for over 38 years, and together they have three beautiful adult children. Denise's desire is to continue her journey in writing Children books that will be an encouragement to all people, especially children. It is her hope to be the best that she can be and encourages others to do the same.

Educator and Children's Book Author

Email: dsstylemarketplace@yahoo.com

website: denisetharpe.my.canva.site

Facebook - Authentic Author Denise Tharpe

901-290-8387

Author
Brittany Morris

Season's
Greetings

Brittany's Books

Brittney Morris is the bestselling author of SLAY, The Cost of Knowing, Marvel's Spider-Man: Miles Morales - Wings of Fury, and The Jump. She also writes video games and has contributed to projects such as The Lost Legends of Redwall, Subnautica: Below Zero, Marvel's Spider-Man 2, and Marvel's Wolverine. Brittney is an NAACP Image Award nominee, an ALA Black Caucus Youth Literary Award winner, and an Ignite Award Finalist. She has an economics degree from Boston University and spends her spare time reading, playing video games, and not doing enough yoga. She lives in Philadelphia.

#1 BEST SELLER

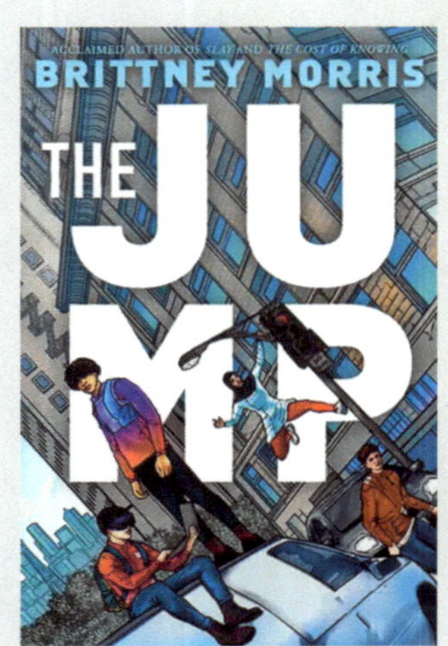

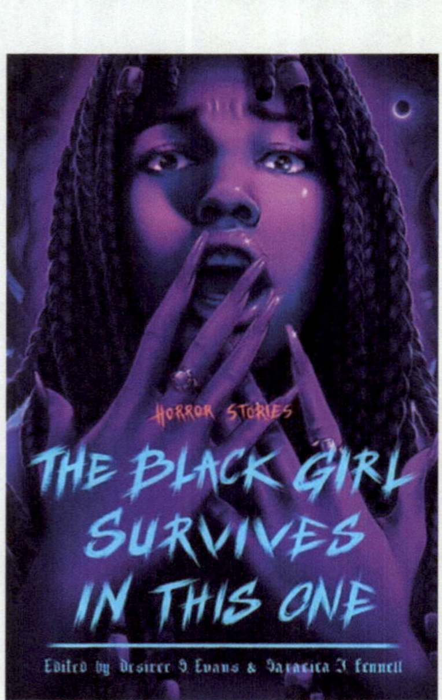

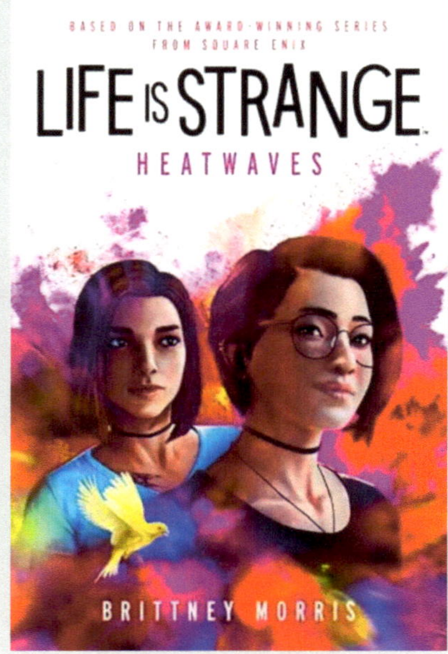

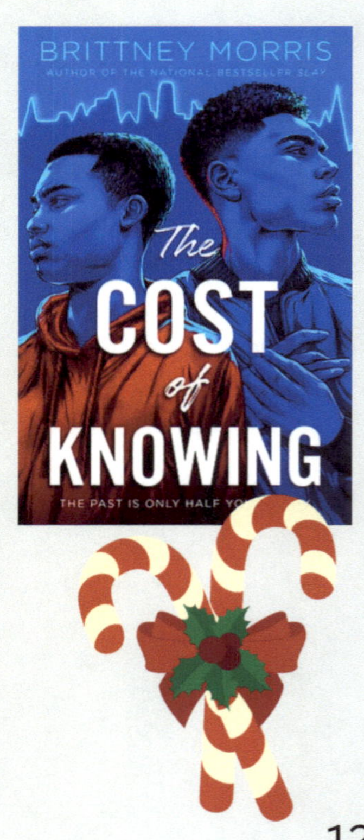

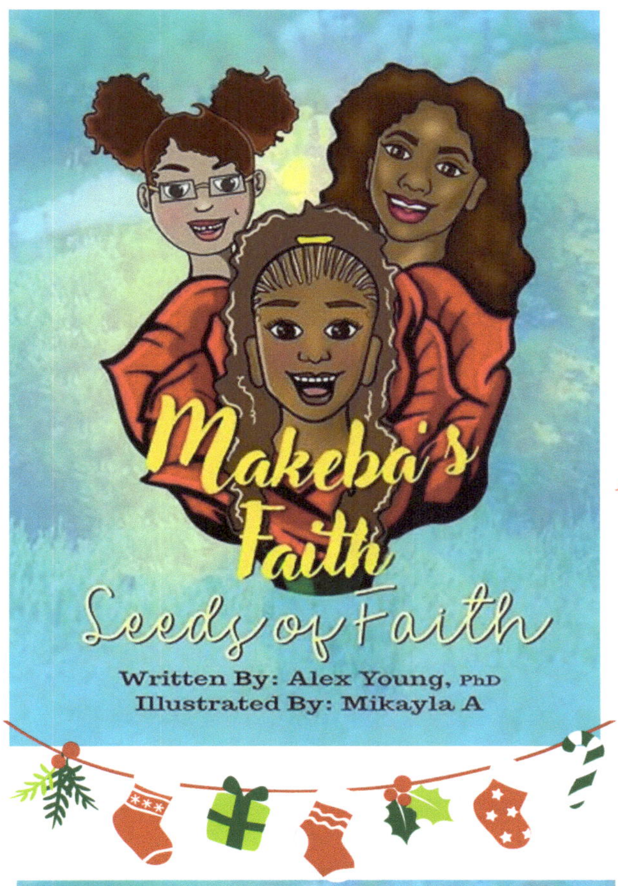

Author Spotlight
Alex Young

Her Book: Makeba's Faith!
Seeds of Faith!

WHAT DOES IT MEAN TO HAVE FAITH? HAVING FAITH AS SMALL AS A SEED CAN DO IMPOSSIBLE THINGS. IN "MAKEBA'S FAITH" BOOK, MAKEBA SHARES HER EXPERIENCE OF HAVING FAITH AS SHE ASSISTS HER FRIEND IN THE GARDEN. THE LESSONS MAKEBA'S MOM INSTILLED IN HER ARE DEMONSTRATED IN HER DAILY ACTIVITIES AND EXPERIENCES.

AUTHOR
Linda Gordon

Dr. Linda R. Gordon, MD, MPH, PMP

Dr. Linda Gordon offers insightful leadership in health strategy development. Her professional experience as a physician and community advocate and her work in the non-profit sector make for informed counsel in child wellness success. With special attention to anxiety, bullying, and faith-based wellness, the services provided include consulting, mental health resource media, and child literature.

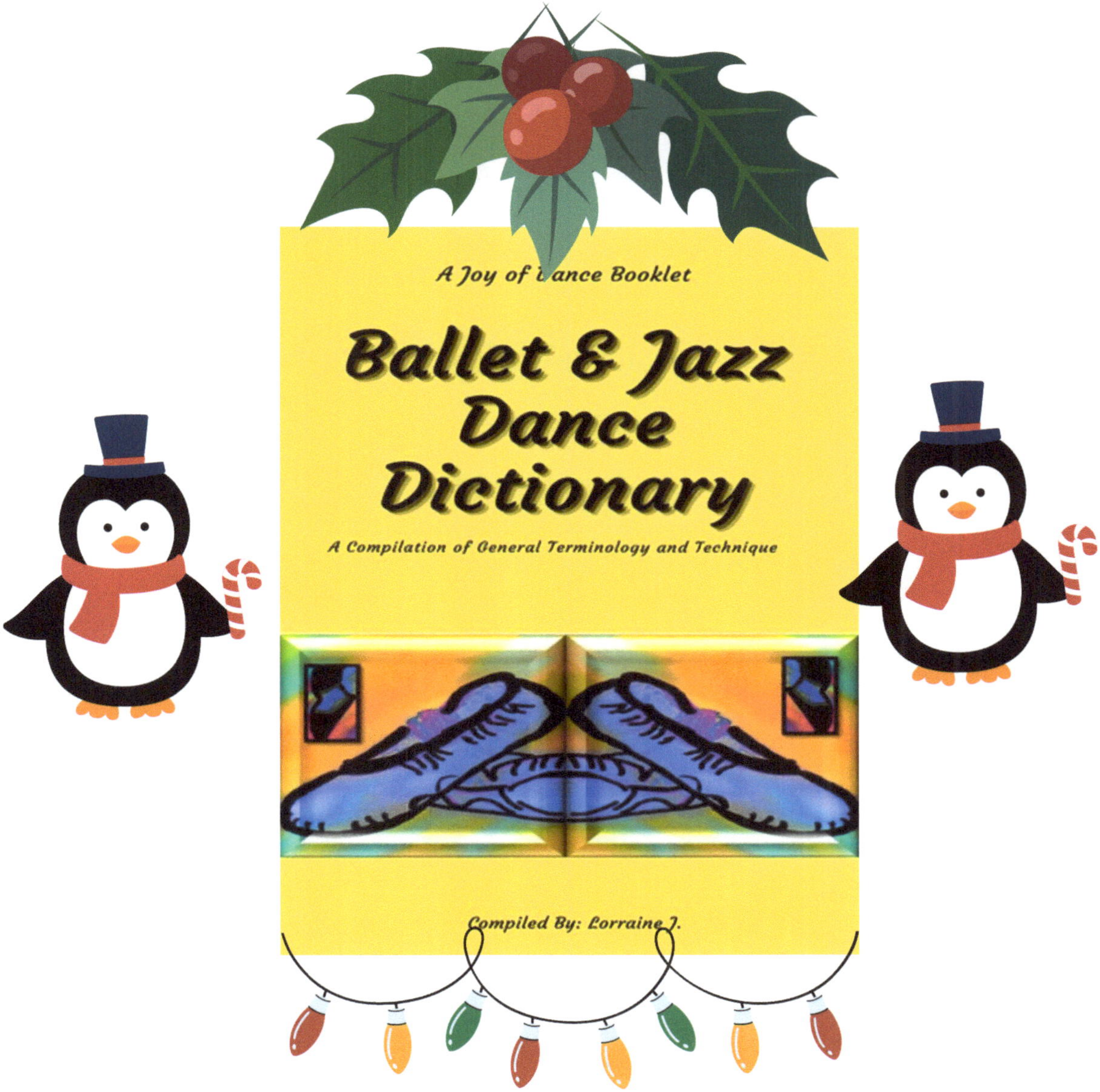

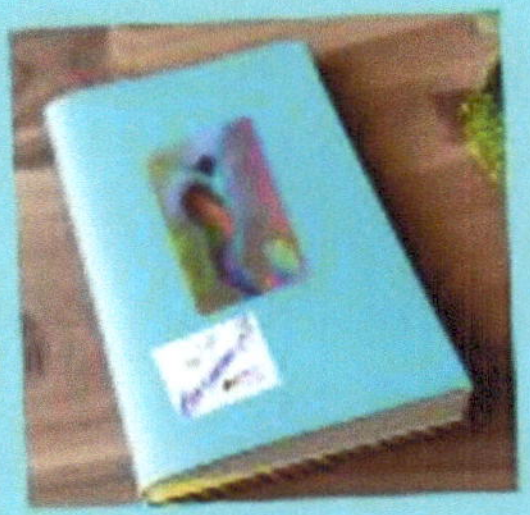

Lorraine Jackson

Author * Writer * Artist

lylte@outlook.com

linktr.ee.lyltexpressions

Author Chilita Faye

About the Author:

Mrs. Chilita Perkins was born and raised in Chicago, Illinois, to Eugene and Vicki Cunningham. From a young age, she was trained for ministerial duties under Elder Titus and the late Virginia Anderson at The Holy Covenant Church of God in Christ. Despite growing up in a home affected by domestic violence, Chilita's mother, an Evangelist at Liberty Tabernacle All Nations Church (LTANC), instilled in her the values and strength needed to stand as a child of God. Following her family's separation from LTANC, Chilita faced numerous challenges and made several life-altering decisions that led her astray. She endured her own battles with domestic violence and family abuse but found solace and focus through activities such as street drill teams and dance groups. On November 24, 1994, Chilita recommitted herself to God at New Birth Outreach Ministry under Pastor Rayford Pointer. By the age of 22, she was ordained as a minister of the gospel. During her time at New Birth Outreach Ministry, Chilita earned a certificate of Training for Service and became a head teacher and organizer for the Children's Ministry and VBS summer programs.

16

Mentored by the head intercessor, Dr. Mildred Harris, Chilita developed into a prayer warrior and a strong, resilient woman. Together with her ex-husband, she engaged in street evangelism and taught evangelism classes to other ministries. Chilita has been recognized for her community activism with medals and certificates from Arnie Duncan of the Chicago Public Schools (CPS) and has served as a community activist for eight years under Developing Community Projects (DCP). She co-founded the Second Chance Organization for the homeless and neglected souls, and established The Vision Dance Production for youth. Additionally, she is a licensed educator, barber, and stylist. As an entrepreneur, she owned several shops titled "Chi Town's Finest Beauty and Barber Shop" in Illinois and Arizona, Currently, she works as a government official. In 2005, Chilita founded Rhema Word Christian Center, where she attended classes on the Apostolic Faith and The School of the Prophets. In 2006, she was called by God as a Prophetess and was later ordained by Apostle Isaac Perkins of Rhema Word Christian Center and Apostle Lopez of Mahanaim New Birth. Prophetess Chilita Perkins is known for her anointing in prophetic worship, deliverance, breakthrough, and restoration under the guidance of the Holy Spirit. She taught and preached the RHEMA WORD of God through prophetic teachings. Through life's challenges, she discovered her true calling as a writer, authoring several books including "Don't Be Afraid to Tell," "The Black Sheep Has Two Faces," "Black America," "Life After Adultery," and her work-in-progress, "Becoming a Woman." Additionally, she is a motivational speaker and social media influencer, hosting a live podcast titled "The Unlocked Chest," featured on Facebook, YouTube, and Instagram. No longer preaching in traditional church settings, Chilita Perkins continues to lead by example, meeting people where they are with truth and respect. She was married to Apostle Isaac Perkins for over 26 years and is a loving mother to three children. One of her sons is a marine. She is grandmother to five grandsons.

Author Spotlight

AUTHORS
SUAD ANDREWS & DASUL ANDREWS

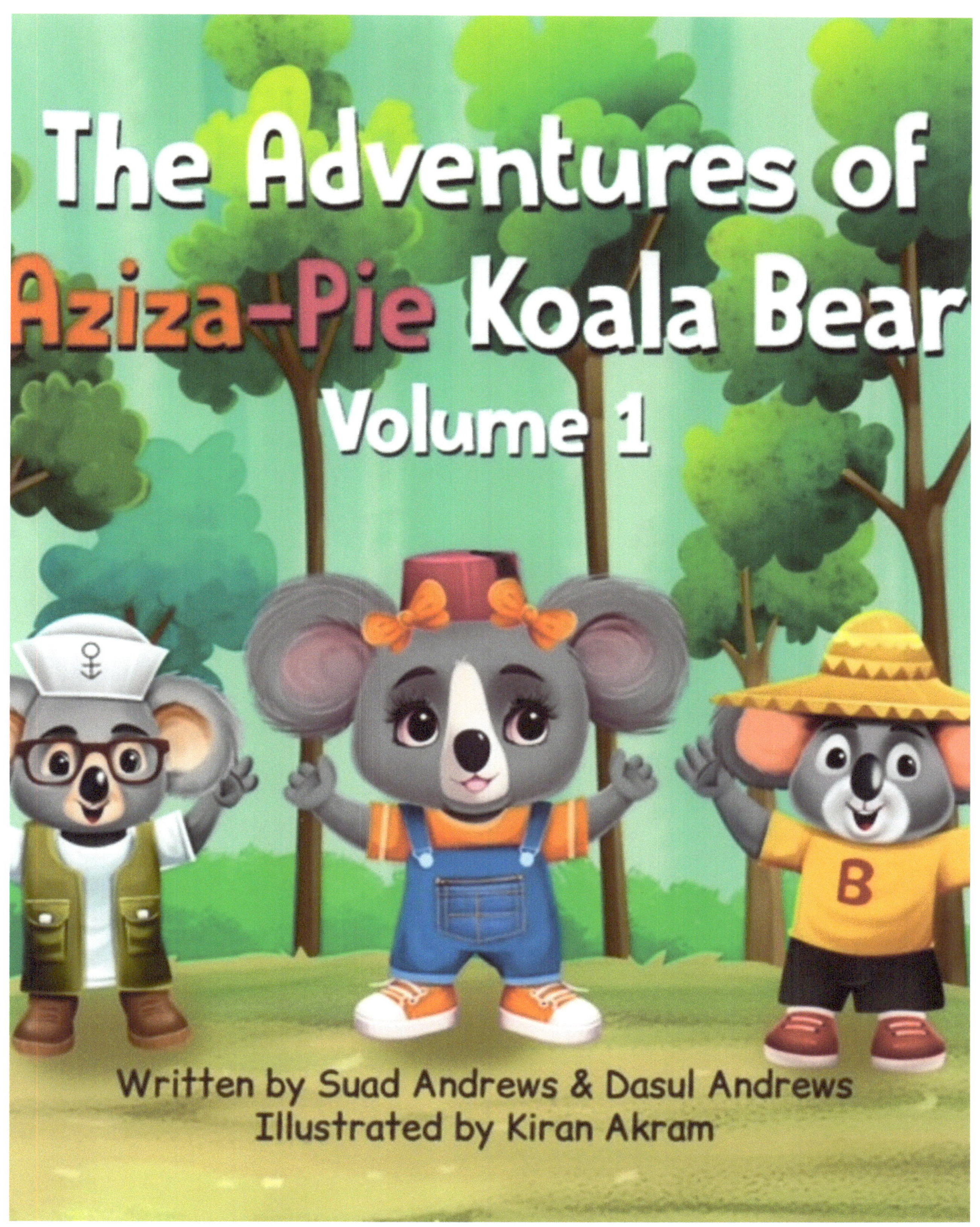

The Adventures of
Aziza-Pie Koala Bear
Volume 1
Written by Suad Andrews & Dasul Andrews
Illustrated by Kiran Akram

About the Author:

In the heartwarming tale of Aziza-Pie Koala Bear, we meet Suad and Dasul Andrews and their daughter, Aziza Denim Andrews. From a young age, Aziza displayed a unique trait her parents called "Koala-ing," symbolizing her strong bond with them.

Born during a global pandemic, Aziza's upbringing was enriched with books and homeschooling, nurturing her vibrant imagination and gifted abilities. Her love for storytelling blossomed during family reading sessions, where she absorbed captivating tales. Recognizing a lack of positive representation in children's literature, Suad inspired Dasul to create change.

Drawing from their family adventures and Aziza's creativity, they set out to craft a world filled with warmth and inclusivity. Aziza-Pie Koala Bear symbolizes the power of imagination, the strength of family ties, and the importance of positive storytelling.

Join us on this enchanting journey and experience the magic of Aziza-Pie Koala Bear— where love, laughter, and endless possibilities await.

2. Book details:

In "The Adventures of Aziza-Pie Koala Bear Volume 1," the heartwarming narrative comes alive as Aziza-Pie's cousins come to visit, transforming an ordinary day into an extraordinary adventure. From the moment they arrive, the air buzzes with laughter and excitement, showcasing the beauty of family love and the joy of togetherness. As they embark on playful escapades, children witnessing this delightful tale will discover not only the thrill of exploration but also the deep-rooted values of kindness and cooperation.

Each activity—from climbing trees to sharing stories under the stars—serves as a reminder that family bonds are woven from shared experiences and mutual support. Aziza-Pie, with her vibrant spirit, encourages her cousins to embrace their individuality while celebrating their connection. The story unfolds with a series of charming adventures, each highlighting the importance of cherishing loved ones and creating lasting memories.

As readers turn each page, they are invited to join Aziza-Pie and her cousins on their journey, igniting their imaginations and inspiring them to seek out their own adventures. Ultimately, this enchanting tale emphasizes that every day is filled with the potential for joy, love, and unforgettable moments with family, making it a truly enriching experience for young readers.

THE ADVENTURES
OF AZIZA-PIE KOALA BEAR

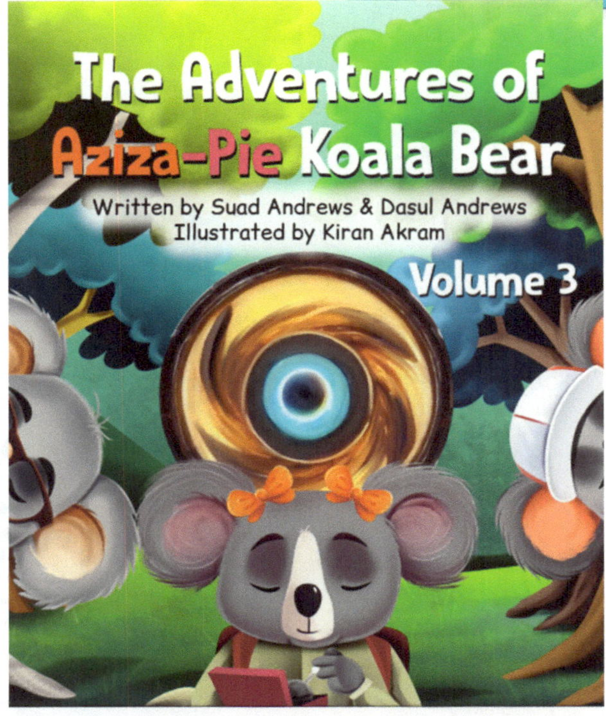

Book Details:

In "The Adventures of Aziza-Pie Koala Bear Volume 1," the heartwarming narrative comes alive as Aziza-Pie's cousins come to visit, transforming an ordinary day into an extraordinary adventure. From the moment they arrive, the air buzzes with laughter and excitement, showcasing the beauty of family love and the joy of togetherness. As they embark on playful escapades, children witnessing this delightful tale will discover not only the thrill of exploration but also the deep-rooted values of kindness and cooperation.

Each activity—from climbing trees to sharing stories under the stars—serves as a reminder that family bonds are woven from shared experiences and mutual support. Aziza-Pie, with her vibrant spirit, encourages her cousins to embrace their individuality while celebrating their connection. The story unfolds with a series of charming adventures, each highlighting the importance of cherishing loved ones and creating lasting memories.

As readers turn each page, they are invited to join Aziza-Pie and her cousins on their journey, igniting their imaginations and inspiring them to seek out their own adventures. Ultimately, this enchanting tale emphasizes that every day is filled with the potential for joy, love, and unforgettable moments with family, making it a truly enriching experience for young readers.

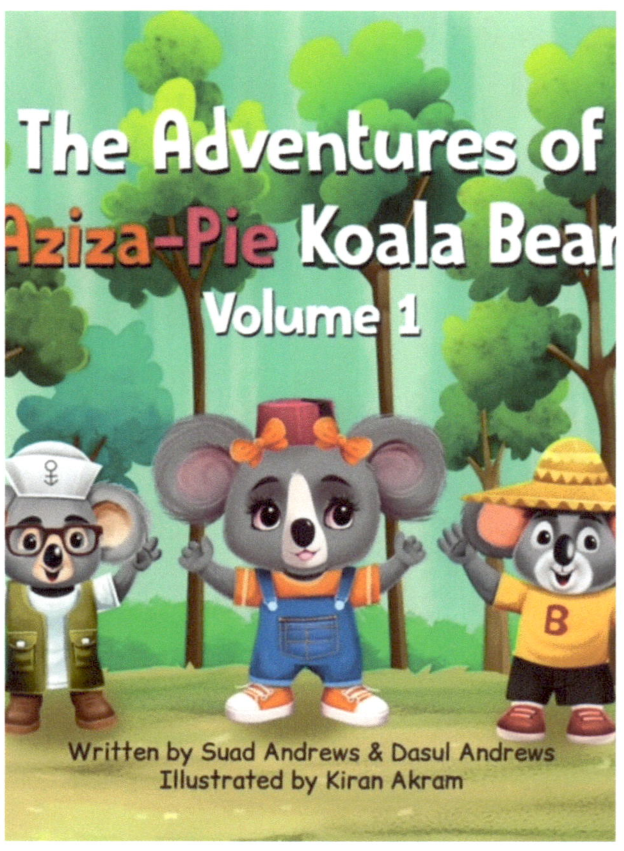

Reading
to
Kids at an early
age
is <u>Priceless!</u>

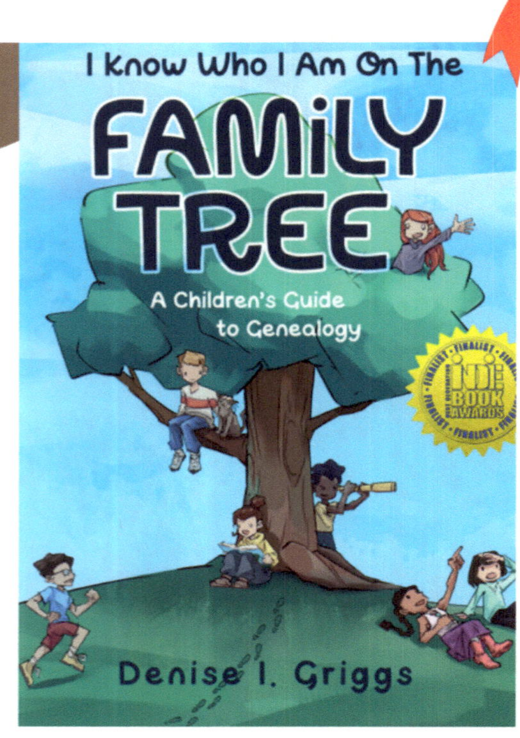

This book will help children and parents work together to uncover facts about their ancestors and how they fit into history, geography, and society. There are gaps in everyone's family history that need to be solved. Some questions might be: Why did families stay where they lived, or why did they suddenly leave? Where did they go? Were they from a large continent or an exotic island? Where does your family name originate? Why do you love certain foods? Where did these foods originate?

Using this book will help locate the clues to answer the history and mysteries of your family. It will help families prepare for the first, or next family reunion!

Author
Denise Griggs

Denise Griggs is a family genealogist with 35 years of research, spanning ancestral roots in diverse countries like Africa, Europe, Australia, Ireland, and North America. Her maternal lineage traces back to eighth-century England and extends to southwest Mississippi.

She discovered the need to teach children the basics of genealogy through her book, I Know Who I Am On the Family Tree, A Children's Guide to Genealogy, for which she earned a Finalist Award in the Indie Book Awards. This work earned her the Next Generation Indie Book Award. Denise is also an author of children's books focusing on diversity and theology.

An advocate for history and heritage, Denise is actively involved in organizations like the Daughters of the American Revolution (DAR), volunteers with the National Park Service, and the Natchez U.S. Colored Troops Monument Committee in Mississippi. She serves as the Exhibit Chair on the board of the Greater Sacramento African American Genealogy Society, preserving and sharing cultural histories. Denise holds honors, with a B.A. and M.A. from a Christian University. She is the owner of Glass Tree Books® and Blue Eclipse Publishing®. Her genealogy presentations are also on her YouTube channel, D.I. Griggs Media.

Navigating the Challenges of Excessive Cell Phone Usage in Teenagers: A Parent's Guide

BY PAULETTE HENSON

As a parent in today's digital world, you've likely witnessed the ever-growing attachment between your teenager and their cell phone. While technology offers numerous benefits, such as staying connected, accessing information, and developing digital skills, excessive cell phone usage can lead to a host of challenges—ranging from academic distractions to social isolation. The question many parents face is: how do we help our teens strike a healthy balance between staying connected and overusing their devices?

Here are some tips for parents to address the issue of excessive cell phone usage and guide teens toward responsible digital habits.

1. Start with Open Communication

Before setting any rules or limits, it's crucial to open a conversation with your teenager about their cell phone usage. Instead of framing it as a problem right away, approach the topic from a place of curiosity and concern.

- Ask open-ended questions: Ask your teen how they feel about their phone use. Are they using it to connect with friends, for entertainment, or to keep up with schoolwork? This can help you understand why they are on their phone so much and guide the discussion.
- Express your concerns calmly: Explain that while cell phones are useful, excessive use may interfere with their focus on academics, sleep, and personal well-being. Make sure they know your concern stems from a desire to help them find balance, not to take away their freedom.

Activities like sports, family night bowling can help minimize cell phone usage.

DESIGNATE PHONE-FREE TIMES!

By fostering an open dialogue, you create a space for your teen to express their thoughts and concerns, making them more likely to collaborate on finding a solution.

2. Set Clear and Realistic Boundaries

Setting boundaries around cell phone use is essential, but they need to be reasonable and realistic. Work with your teen to create guidelines that they understand and can follow.

- Designate "phone-free" times: Establish periods during the day when cell phones are not allowed, such as during family meals, homework time, or before bed. This can help your teen focus on schoolwork, family interactions, and rest without distractions.
- Limit screen time: Create a daily limit on how much time your teen can spend on non-school-related activities on their phone. Many smartphones have built-in features that track screen time and can set daily limits for specific apps.
- Device-free zones: Consider designating certain areas of the house, like the dining room or bedrooms, as "device-free zones" to encourage more meaningful interactions and better sleep habits.
- Make sure to explain the reasoning behind each rule, and whenever possible, include your teen in the decision-making process. This gives them a sense of responsibility and ownership over the guidelines.

- **3. Encourage Offline Activities**
- Teenagers often turn to their phones for entertainment, connection, or boredom relief. Help them find engaging alternatives that don't involve a screen.
- Promote hobbies and interests: Encourage your teen to explore activities they enjoy, such as playing a sport, reading, drawing, or joining a club. These hobbies can offer a fulfilling and screen-free outlet for their energy and creativity.
- Family time: Plan regular family outings or game nights where everyone, including you, is off their phones. This allows for quality time together and sets an example of balancing screen time with personal interactions.
- Encourage in-person socializing: If your teen is glued to their phone to stay in touch with friends, suggest they meet up in person whenever possible. In-person interactions can help improve their social skills and build deeper connections.
- By promoting engaging offline activities, you offer your teen alternatives that keep them connected to the real world without relying solely on their phone.
- **4. Model Healthy Behavior**
- Children and teens often mimic the behavior of their parents, whether it's positive or negative. If they see you frequently checking your phone during conversations or at the dinner table, they may see excessive cell phone use as acceptable.

Lead by example: Practice the same phone boundaries you set for your teen. For example, if you've agreed on no phones during meals, make sure you're following that rule, too. By modeling balanced phone usage, you're showing your teen that it's possible—and beneficial—to disconnect from screens.

Schedule screen breaks: Take breaks from your own devices and spend that time with your teen. Go for a walk, play a board game, or cook a meal together. This shows that you value time spent together without digital distractions.

5. Be Aware of the Risks

Excessive cell phone usage can lead to more than just a distracted teen. There are potential risks associated with too much screen time that can affect both their mental and physical well-being.

Mental health impacts: Excessive phone use, especially on social media, can lead to issues like anxiety, depression, and low self-esteem. Teens may compare themselves to others online, leading to feelings of inadequacy.

Sleep disruption: The blue light emitted by phones can interfere with your teen's ability to fall asleep and stay asleep. Encourage them to avoid phone usage at least an hour before bedtime to promote better rest.

Academic performance: Constant texting, scrolling, or gaming can distract your teen from their studies, leading to lower grades and difficulty concentrating.

Discuss these risks with your teen and explain how moderate phone usage can help protect their health, both mentally and physically.

6. Use Technology for Good

While the goal is to manage excessive use, not all phone use is bad. There are ways to harness the power of technology to benefit your teen's education and personal growth.

Educational apps: Encourage your teen to download apps that support learning, such as language learning apps, math games, or apps that teach coding or other valuable skills.

Time management tools: Many smartphones offer time-tracking features that can help teens monitor their screen time. Teach your teen how to use these tools to become more aware of their usage habits and to set personal goals for managing their time better.

Positive online communities: Help your teen identify online communities or social platforms that support their interests in a positive being.

and constructive way. For example, they can join a book club, engage with art communities, or participate in educational forums.

7. Be Patient and Consistent

Changing habits takes time. If your teen has been using their phone excessively, it may take a while to break the cycle. Be patient as they adjust to new rules and limits, and remain consistent in enforcing boundaries.

Avoid punishments: Instead of using phone restrictions as a form of punishment, try to maintain an open and supportive dialogue about why limits are important.

Celebrate successes: When your teen follows the rules, give them positive reinforcement. Praise them for balancing their phone use with their other responsibilities, which will encourage them to continue the good behavior.

In today's digital age, balancing cell phone usage is a challenge for both teens and parents. By approaching the issue with open communication, clear boundaries, and a positive, supportive attitude, you can help your teen develop healthy digital habits. Remember, the goal isn't to eliminate phones altogether but to guide your teen toward responsible and balanced usage that benefits their overall well-

Author
Lena Lee

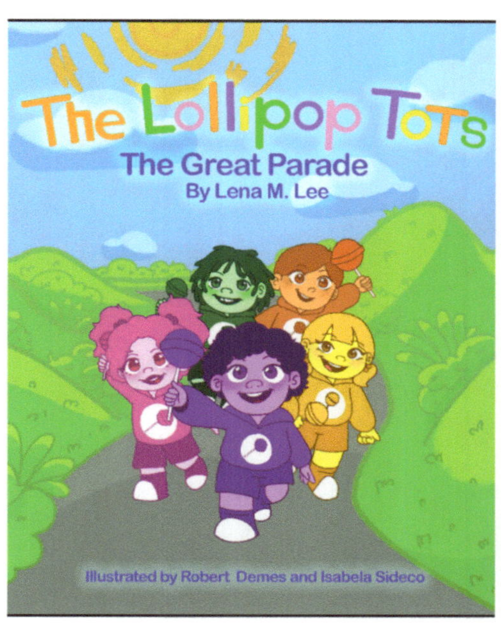

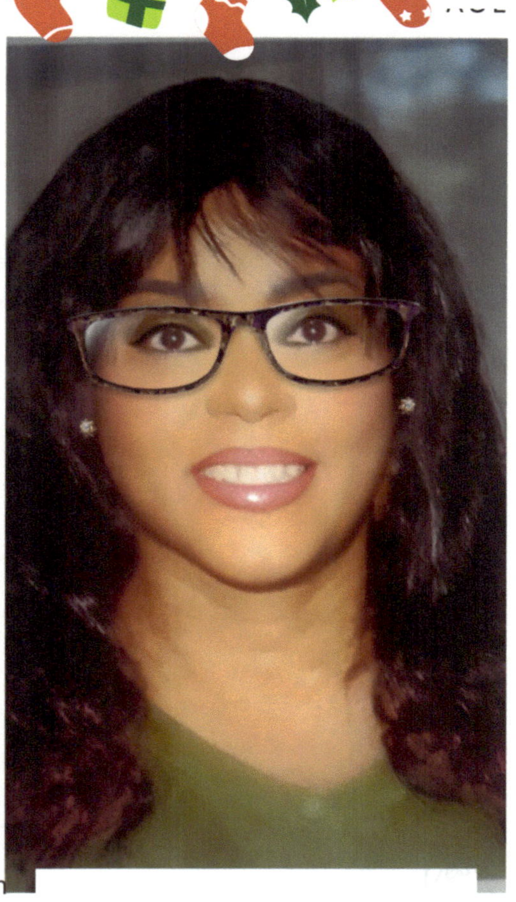

LENA M. LEE, a native of southeastern Pennsylvania developed her love for writing, art, fashion and inventions at an early age. In 2000, Lee was awarded a utility patent for dolls she created that were of no race or nationality for both boys and girls called "The Lollipop Tots" and has written 16 short stories about the dolls. Her first published of the series, The Lollipop Tots -The Great Parade. She is also the published author of "Panic in the Jungle" and has a patent pending for a multifunctional laptop invention which she won first place at West Chester University in 2014 for most innovative new idea. In her spare time, Lee enjoys reading, drawing and spending time with her family.

Featured Author
Chantelle
Crowell

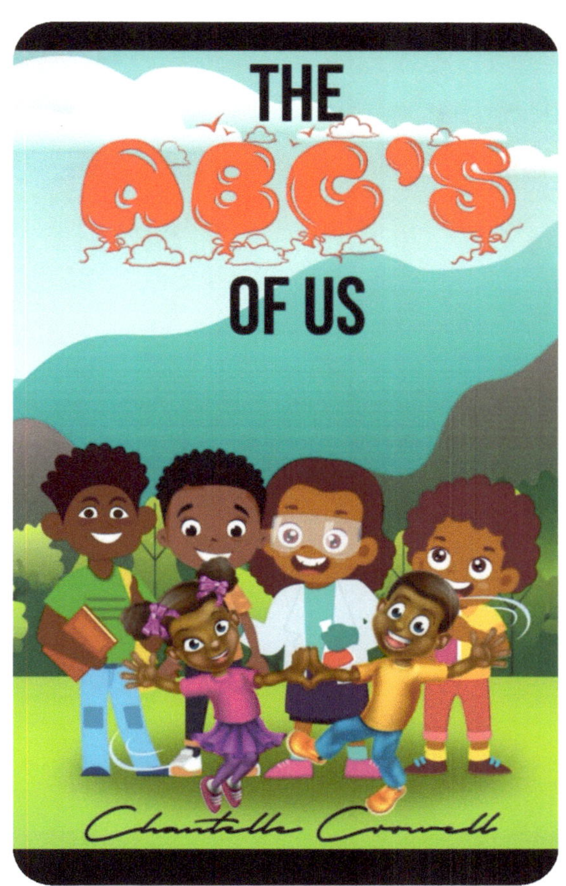

Author Chantelle Crowell

Ms. Chantelle Crowell is an accomplished African-American author and devoted mother, having written twelve books with more on the way. A graduate of Central Piedmont Community College, she skillfully balances her successful writing career with caring for her family. Her work is celebrated for its authenticity and deep connection to her experiences, inspiring readers across generations. She draws inspiration from her life, weaving themes of family, resilience, and culture into her narratives. Her commitment to storytelling and her community has made her a beloved figure among her readers and peers.

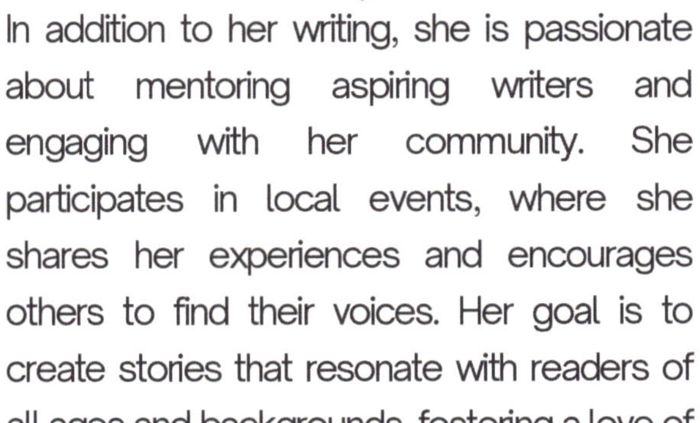

In addition to her writing, she is passionate about mentoring aspiring writers and engaging with her community. She participates in local events, where she shares her experiences and encourages others to find their voices. Her goal is to create stories that resonate with readers of all ages and backgrounds, fostering a love of literature and lifelong learning.

We Wake Up is a beautifully crafted children's book that invites readers to explore a vibrant world while emphasizing the importance of lending a helping hand to others. *Journey*, one of my personal favorites, is inspired by a close friend, a talented blues reggae artist. This book encourages readers to follow their own path, dance to the beat of their own drum, and with focus, courage, and perseverance, turn their dreams into reality. *We Are the Revolution* empowers readers to embrace their thoughts, feelings, and emotions. It guides them on a journey of self-discovery, reminding them that their voice can make an impact even without a microphone. *The Big Brown Box* takes readers on a delightful musical adventure, exploring the unique sounds of different instruments while showing that there's joy to be found in creativity and play. *The Candy Cane Dance* is a heartwarming holiday story that brings people together for a festive dance, complete with a special guest appearance and a sweet treat at the end. *Mr. Biggles and the Garden* tells the story of how friendships can blossom while working together to care for the environment, emphasizing the importance of teamwork and community. *Where Are My Socks?* is a charming tale about a boy and his dog, as they embark on a playful adventure in search of the boy's missing socks. *No Tricks, Just Treats* brings the magic of Halloween to life, following a young girl who eagerly anticipates the holiday fun with friends, along with the excitement of collecting treats. *The Thanksgiving Turkey* puts a unique spin on the traditional holiday feast, with an unexpected twist that makes readers reconsider the meaning of Thanksgiving. *The ABC's of Us* is a collection of inspiring and descriptive words that celebrate the uniqueness in all of us, offering encouragement and affirming that everyone is special. Finally, *Alkebu-lan* is a generational story of strength and resilience, showcasing how one family's enduring support for each other has carried them through challenges, a legacy that continues today.

Chantelle's Books

The Big Brown Box, offers a touch of musical mystery. It aims to ignite your curiosity about music, just as it did for me and my older brothers. Inspired by my brothers' enjoyment of playing various instruments, this book explores the magic of discovering new sounds.

The ABCs of Us, focuses on celebrating who we are. It features inspirational and descriptive words that highlight our qualities and strengths. This book aims to demonstrate how we can uplift ourselves and support each other.

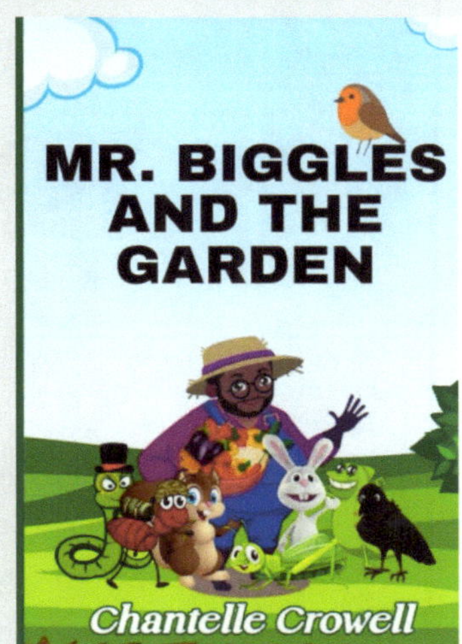

The Thanksgiving Turkey, illustrates that even with hard work and preparation, unexpected challenges can arise. When this happens, you must find a way to overcome them. This humorous story is sure to make you smile.

Mr.Biggles in the Garden, features a character inspired by one of my older brothers. He encouraged me to write about a gardener and his garden and the support he receives from unusual friends.

Chantelle's Books

No Tricks, Just Treats, tells the story of a little girl who delights in her beloved holiday. She involves her mother in a special task, which they complete together, and then she goes out to celebrate with her friends.

Where Are My Socks?, was co-written by my youngest son and I. The inspiration for this book came from two sources: my youngest son, who is always searching for his favorite pair of socks, and our family dog. The story captures the obstacles my son faces in his quest to find his socks.

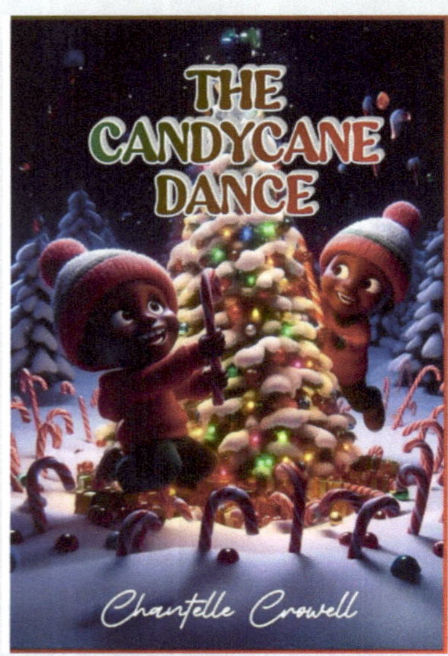

The Candy Cane Dance, is about enjoying a festive Christmas dance and taking home a special treat. It features a special guest and shows how all the students come together to celebrate and have fun.

Journey, focuses on inspiration. It motivates you to pursue your own path, embrace your individuality, and overcome any obstacles while staying dedicated to your dreams and achieving them.

Literary
MOMENTS & RESOURCES

A One-Stop Shop
For Authors

AUTHORPRENEURSHIP 101 COURSE FOR AUTHORS!

- **A GUIDED COURSE TO HELP YOU COMPLETE & PUBLISH YOUR BOOK**
- **CLASSES BEGIN – JAN 2025**

REGISTER:EDUCATION@BLACKWOMENAUTHORS.NET

Lead by Prof. Paulette Henson and Michelle Hardy (@SolitudeWithMichelle)

At BWA, our goal is to educate new and blossoming writers on how to write and publish books.

Whether you are just budding, wanting to finally complete a writing project, or already seasoned, we're more than happy to help you on your journey from writing to publishing your book.

BWA proudly announces its first course to help our strong community build the best possible quality book for its members and their target audience. Author Preneurship 101 taught by Professor Paulette Henson and Michelle Hardy is an author business writing course designed to help new and seasoned authors get published in a one-stop shop. Being a new author can be challenging, but BWA is here to make things go as smoothly as possible with a complete writing and publishing process.

For information or to register send an email to:

Education@blackwomenauthors.net

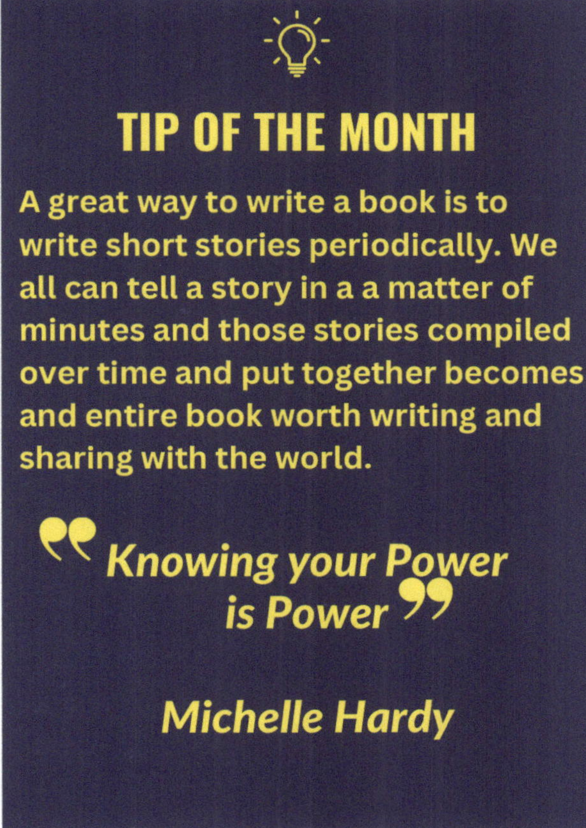

We Help
You Promote Your Business & Books

PUBLICATION & MARKETING COMPANY

SERVICES

Book Promotion & Strategy
Marketing in one of our monthly BWA publications.

Digital Book & Author Development
Website Design & Development
Book Trailers
Print to Ebook Conversion

Education & Resources
New Author Course & Workshop
Online Courses for Seasoned Authors

ABOUT US

We are committed to being the primary resource for Authors to succeed in their Book Promotions.

WHY CHOOSE US ?

We are the only Black Owned platform providing this level of resource and service.

CONTACT

BWAMAGAZINE@GMAIL.COM

blackwomenauthors.net

As the end of the year approaches, the holiday season brings with it a time of reflection, renewed connection, and hopeful anticipation. At the heart of this special time lies the spiritual meaning that transcends any single religion or cultural tradition.

The essence of the holidays is the spirit of loving one another. Whether it's the Christian celebration of Christmas, the African American tradition of Kwanzaa, or the universal joy of welcoming a new year, the common thread is an emphasis on community, compassion, and our shared humanity.

During Christmas, the birth of Jesus Christ symbolizes the divine gift of unconditional love. Kwanzaa honors the seven principles of African heritage, including unity, self-determination, and faith. And as we say goodbye to the old year, the arrival of a new one represents an opportunity for fresh starts and bold resolutions.

Across these diverse observances, the holiday spirit encourages us to look beyond our differences and find common ground. It's a chance to slow down, express gratitude, and recommit ourselves to the values that truly matter - kindness, generosity, and the belief that we are all connected.

As 2024 draws to a close, the spiritual meaning of the season invites us to reflect on the year gone by. What lessons have we learned? How can we grow and improve in the years ahead? By tapping into the universal themes of light, renewal, and goodwill, we can enter 2025 with a sense of purpose and optimism. This is the perfect time to set meaningful goals for the new year - whether it's practicing more mindfulness, volunteering in our communities, or finding innovative ways to make a positive impact. When we approach the future with open hearts and a genuine commitment to one another, we unlock the fullest expression of the holiday spirit.

No matter our faith or background, the end-of-year festivities remind us that we are all part of the human family. As we celebrate and look forward, may we carry this sense of connection, compassion, and hope with us, not just for the holidays, but throughout the year to come.

P.K. Wilson

Good Health!

BWA *go*

COMING SOON...

Book All Your Travel Needs - In One Spot!

FLIGHTS - HOTELS - CAR RENTALS
CRUISES - VACATION PACKAGES

- BUSINESS & PERSONAL TRAVEL
- FAMILY/HOLIDAY EVENTS
- BOOK FAIRS
- ADVENTURE TRAVEL
- SPECIAL & CUSTOM PACKAGES

Priceless Little Things!

Just staying busy in the day-to-day, I became remiss about how much our babies and small people mimic what we do. Their minds are constantly recording what we do, how we say, how we act, our tone, and so on. Lucky for me, I am a positive person, most of my habits are good, and most of the time I know they're watching me (and learning).

Kids love to have a book read to them. Read to them with enthusiasm and expression as much as possible. Then, later, ask them simple questions about the story, like what was his/her name? Or, why did that happen?

I remember reading the three little pigs to my sons when they were toddlers. I used different voices for each pig, and another voice for the big bad wolf. Then I would re-read the book while pointing at the words so they also recognized sight words. Soon enough it was easy for them to read a story back to me.
Nowadays, I let my one-year-old granddaughter walk around the library freely in the sections appropriate for her age. I'll point at a familiar book and ask her "what's that one"?

Forgetting about her 'inside' library voice she'll turn to me and yell out whatever the story is, mimicking the full effects of the voices in the story. She is eager to let me know she knows the story, even though her vocabulary is primarily baby words.
Now, the lesson here is to always be mindful that these small people are recording and mimicking everything. They develop excellent reading habits and a love for books. This is good.

The best part of this short story is my one-year-old granddaughter now has a new baby sister who is only a few months old. It is priceless to hear the toddler telling stories to the new baby, albeit in her own baby speak, mimicking the same voices and sounds that I make.

You can't put a price on that!

By A. Williams

The Author's Lounge W/PAULETTE

Next Guest Author: You!

PROMOTE YOUR BOOK !

FOR MORE DETAILS

EMAIL:THEAUTHORSLOUNGETVSHOW@GMAIL.COM

WATCH ON FACEBOOK
(LIVE) BLACK WOMEN
AUTHORS
& YOUTUBE

LIKE/COMMENT/SHARE/SUBSCRIBE

Why Road Trips are the Perfect Opportunity for Activity Books and Reading

By Paulette Henson

Let's Go!

There's something magical about hitting the open road—long stretches of highway, scenic views, and the anticipation of arriving at your destination. For families, road trips offer a unique chance to bond, explore new places, and make lasting memories. However, for parents, the long hours in the car with restless children can be a challenge. That's where activity books and reading come to the rescue!

Bringing along books, activity pads, and engaging stories can not only keep your kids entertained during a road trip, but also encourage their love for reading and learning. Here's why road trips are a fantastic time to introduce activity books and reading to your children, and some tips on how to make the most of it.

1. A Break from Screens

In today's digital age, kids spend much of their time glued to screens—whether it's watching TV, playing games on tablets, or scrolling through their phones. Road trips offer the perfect opportunity to give them a break from screens and introduce more hands-on, engaging activities.

Activity books: Coloring books, puzzle books, or sticker activity pads can captivate children's imaginations and keep them occupied for hours. Whether it's solving mazes, matching games, or completing simple math problems, these activities sharpen their minds without the need for electronics.

Reading: Car rides are a great time to enjoy a good book. For younger children, picture books with vibrant illustrations can spark curiosity, while older kids can dive into chapter books that whisk them away to new worlds, all while they're buckled up and watching the road go by.

Taking a break from screens not only reduces eye strain but also fosters creativity and imagination as your children explore stories and activities in the car.

2. Encouraging a Love for Reading

The uninterrupted hours of a road trip provide an ideal setting for reading. With no distractions from TV shows, video games, or friends, kids can immerse themselves in the joy of storytelling.

Storytime in the car: For younger children who can't read on their own yet, parents can read aloud from a favorite book. This can create a bonding moment for the entire family and make the hours in the car fly by. Choose a fun, family-friendly book that everyone will enjoy!

Audiobooks: Audiobooks are another great option, especially for longer trips. Listening to a well-narrated story together can turn a road trip into an exciting adventure. Whether it's a classic children's tale or a modern series, audiobooks can stimulate children's imaginations and enhance their listening skills.

By incorporating reading into road trips, parents can foster a lifelong love for books and stories in their children.

3. Keeping Minds Active on the Road

Long car rides can sometimes feel like wasted time, but with the right materials, your kids can be learning and growing without even realizing it. Activity books and reading help keep their minds sharp and active, turning the road trip into an educational experience.

Activity books for learning: Whether it's math, language arts, or science, there are plenty of educational activity books designed to make learning fun. You can choose books with activities that match your child's interests or subjects they might need extra practice in. For example, a travel-themed activity book could include geography quizzes or maps to track your journey.

Enhancing vocabulary through reading: Reading during a road trip is a fantastic way to expand your child's vocabulary. Whether they're reading independently or listening to a story, they'll be exposed to new words and phrases, which will help improve their language skills.

Road trips don't have to be downtime—they can be an opportunity for learning and growth in a fun, relaxed environment.

4. Creating Memories Through Stories

Part of what makes road trips special is the chance to create lasting memories. Adding books and stories into the mix can enhance these memories and give children something to associate with the trip.

Themed books: One fun idea is to choose books or activity pads that are related to your destination. Heading to the beach? Pack books about ocean life, pirates, or beach adventures. Going to the mountains? Bring along stories of forest animals or hiking adventures. These thematic books help your child connect their reading with the real-world experiences they'll encounter on the trip.

Journals and scrapbooks: Encourage your child to create a travel journal or scrapbook to document their road trip. They can write about the places they visit, draw pictures of what they see, or even stick in souvenirs like postcards or pressed flowers. This not only promotes writing and creative expression but also helps them build lasting memories from the trip.

Books and activities that are connected to the adventure make the road trip more engaging and exciting for children.

5. Tips for Road Trip Reading and Activities

Here are a few tips to help you successfully incorporate reading and activity books into your next family road trip:

Pack a variety: Bring a mix of books, including picture books, chapter books, and activity books, to suit different moods. Variety keeps things fresh and ensures there's always something new to explore.

Use travel-themed books: Choose books that fit with the theme of your trip, like nature-themed stories for a camping trip or historical tales for a visit to a landmark.

Create a book rotation: If you have multiple children, let them take turns choosing a book or activity. This ensures everyone gets a say and makes the trip more inclusive and fun.

Prepare a travel book bag: Pack a special bag filled with reading and activity materials that are only for the road trip. When kids know the items are just for the trip, they'll be more excited to use them.

Take breaks: If your child is prone to carsickness, take regular breaks from reading. During rest stops, encourage them to stretch their legs and play games that don't involve screens or books, giving them a balanced experience.

6. Turn the Car into a Learning Hub

With a little preparation, your road trip can be more than just a way to get from point A to point B—it can become a mobile learning hub for your kids. By combining the power of reading, storytelling, and creative activities, you'll help your children expand their minds and make the journey as rewarding as the destination.

Incorporating activity books and reading into your road trip routine is a win-win for both parents and kids. It not only keeps children engaged and entertained but also enriches their learning experiences. So, the next time you plan a road trip, don't forget to pack plenty of books and activity pads. They'll turn the drive into an adventure in itself—one filled with fun, learning, and creativity!

Sweet & Healthy Treats
For The Holidays

#1 Classic Christmas Sugar Cookies

1. Classic Christmas Sugar Cookies
Ingredients:
2 ¾ cups all-purpose flour
1 teaspoon baking powder
½ teaspoon baking soda
1 cup unsalted butter, softened
1 ½ cups granulated sugar
1 egg
1 teaspoon vanilla extract
½ teaspoon almond extract
1 tablespoon milk
Colored sugar or sprinkles (optional)
Frosting (optional)
Instructions:
In a medium bowl, whisk together flour, baking powder, and baking soda.
In a large bowl, cream together the butter and sugar until light and fluffy. Beat in the egg, vanilla, and almond extract. Gradually add in the flour mixture and milk until a dough forms.
Preheat the oven to 375°F (190°C). Roll dough into 1-inch balls, place on ungreased cookie sheets, and gently flatten each with the bottom of a glass.
Bake for 8-10 minutes until the edges are just lightly golden. Let cool on the baking sheet for a few minutes, then transfer to a wire rack.
Decorate with frosting, colored sugar, or sprinkles.
Description of Image: A plate of golden sugar cookies decorated with festive frosting designs, topped with green and red sprinkles.

#2 Snowman Banana Pops

A fun, healthy treat that's as adorable as it is delicious!

Ingredients:

2 large bananas

6 pretzel sticks

6 mini chocolate chips (for eyes and buttons)

3 orange candy-coated chocolates (for noses)

3 popsicle sticks

1 cup Greek yogurt (optional for dipping)

Instructions:

Peel the bananas and cut each in half. Insert a popsicle stick into the flat end of each banana half.

Optional: Dip the bananas in Greek yogurt to make them look like frosty snowmen. Place on a baking sheet lined with parchment paper.

Use mini chocolate chips to create eyes and buttons, and add an orange candy for the nose.

Break pretzel sticks in half and insert them into the banana sides as arms.

Freeze for 2-3 hours or until firm. Serve and enjoy!

#3 Christmas Tree Fruit Skewers

A colorful and festive treat that kids will love!

Ingredients:

1 green apple

1 red apple

1 bunch of green grapes

1 cup strawberries (hulled and halved)

6 small star-shaped cookie cutters (or pre-cut star-shaped fruit)

6 wooden skewers

Instructions:

Slice the green apple and red apple into thin rounds. Use a small star-shaped cookie cutter to cut star shapes from the slices.

On each skewer, layer a grape, a strawberry half, and an alternating mix of grape and apple stars.

Top the skewer with a green apple star to resemble a Christmas tree.

Serve immediately or refrigerate until ready to eat.

These treats are perfect for a holiday party or a fun family activity!

Fun Activities ↘
for Youth

Find Your Way out!

ages 8-12

Find the Cheese

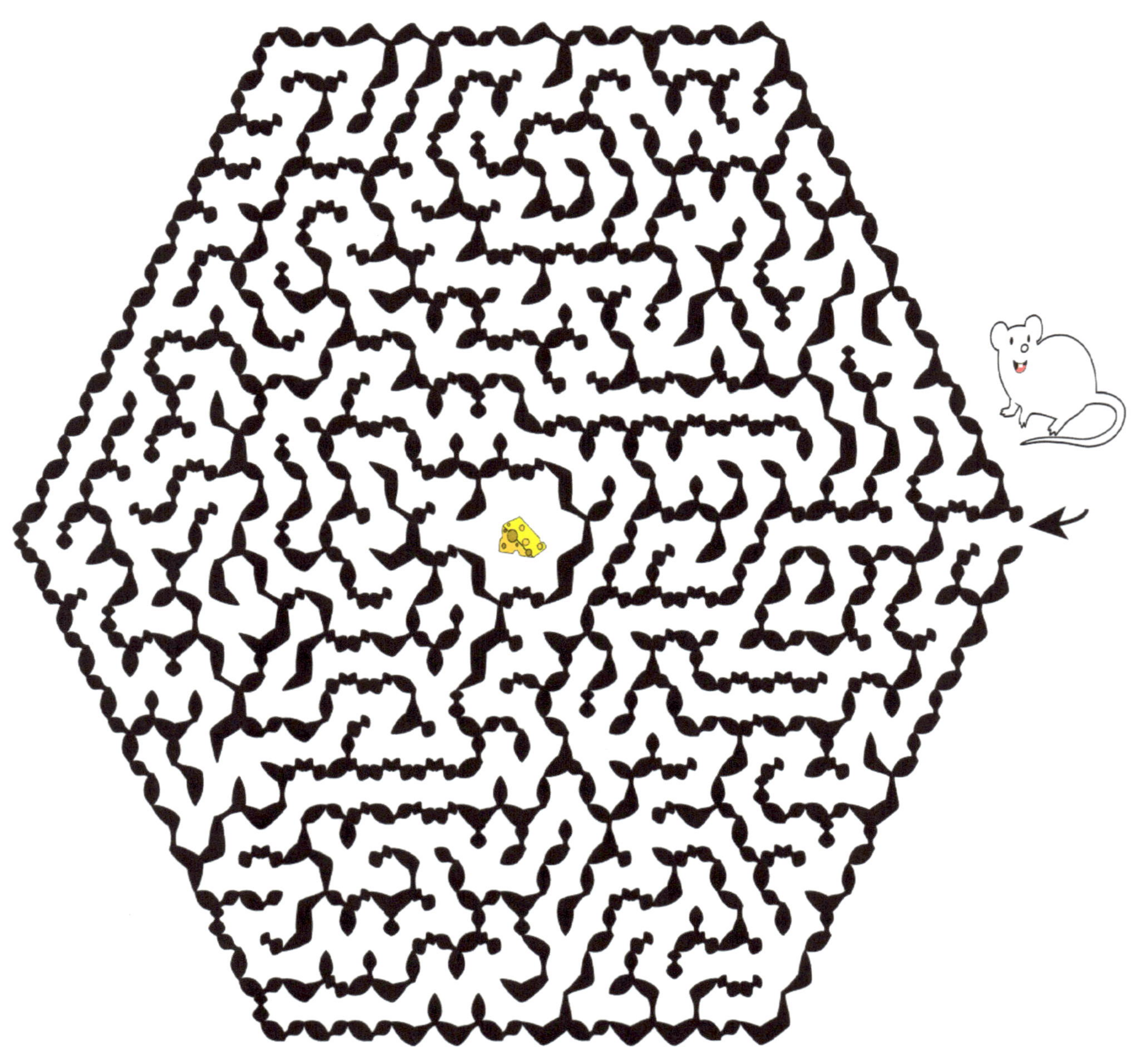

Find your way out
ages 17 & up

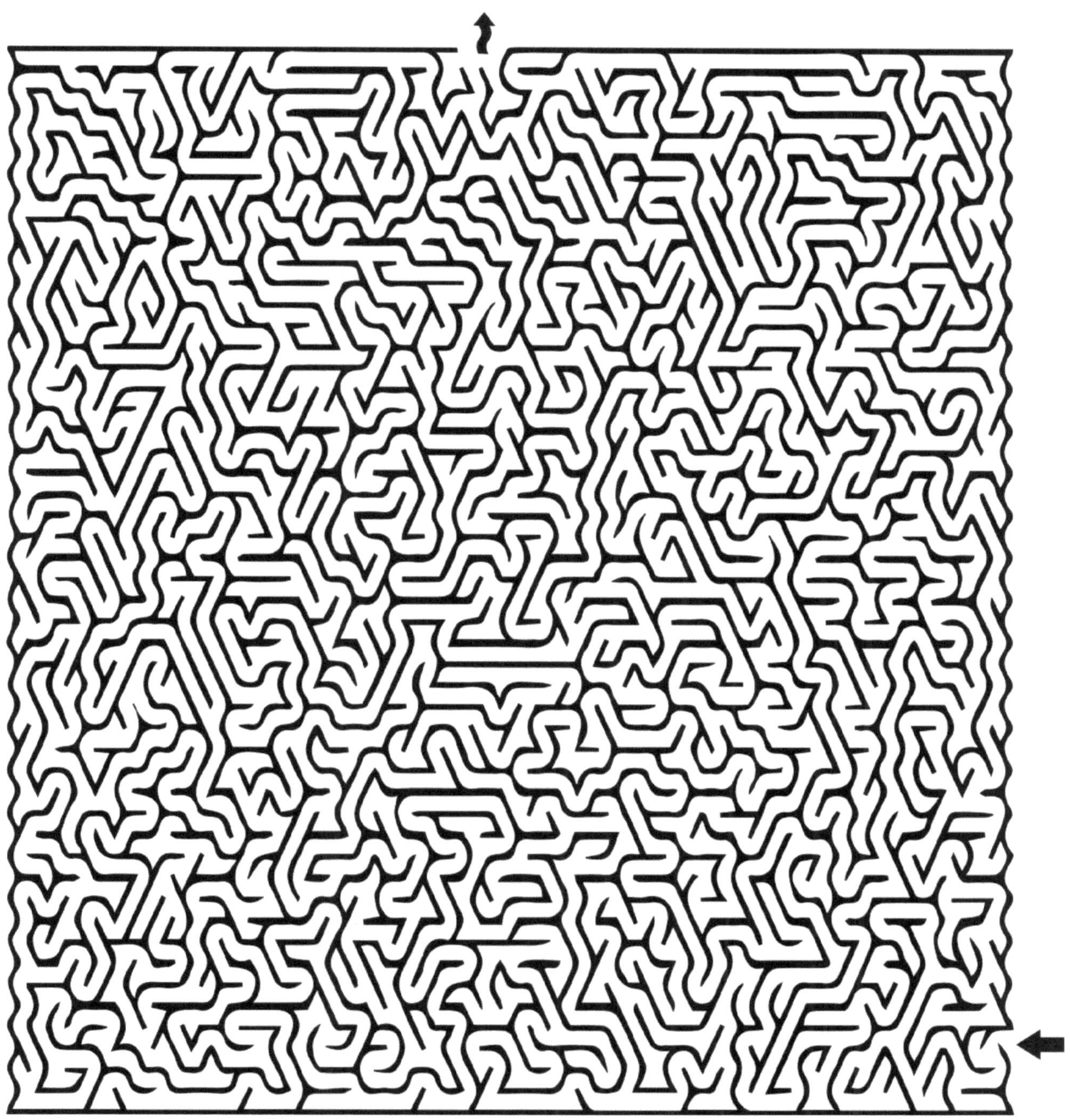

The Game of Life: How Video Games Are Changing Our World

By Victoria H. Pearson July 1, 2024

As a mother of two children born in the mid-90s and a technology professional at the forefront of.

When screens, video games, and constant internet access began their takeover in the early 2000s, I made deliberate choices for my family. From the outset, television was a controlled commodity in our home - a weekend treat, not a daily staple, and always a shared experience rather than a solo escape. This approach extended naturally to video games as they entered the scene.

Our home was always a sanctuary of books, puzzles, "science" projects, outdoor adventures, and creative pursuits. As my children grew older, their introduction to video games was carefully curated - think Mario Brothers, not violent shooters - and always as a shared activity with family. Screen time, whether TV or games, was a weekend only reward, ending Sunday at noon, only after homework was completed.

This wasn't just about restricting digital entertainment; it was about fostering cognitive development, encouraging real-world social skills, and nurturing creativity in a world increasingly dominated by pixels and virtual interactions. My professional background gave me a unique perspective on the potential of these technologies, while my role as a mother drove me to find a balanced approach to their use.

These experiences - as a tech professional and a mindful parent - ignited a deep interest in how gaming and gamification are reshaping our world, particularly for African American communities. They've given me a nuanced understanding of both the promise and the pitfalls of our increasingly gamified society.

American women, we're in a special position – we've seen this change happen, and now we can guide the next generation.

The idea of "gamification" – using elements from games in non-game situations has spread far beyond just playing for fun. From schools to offices, from fitness apps to community projects, game-like features are being used to grab attention and get people involved. But what does this mean for our communities, our families, and our personal growth?

The Video Game Generation

The first generation to grow up surrounded by video games is now becoming adults. These "digital natives" have been shaped by constantly interacting with systems that give quick rewards. A study by the Pew Research Center found that 90% of teens play video games, with little difference between genders, races, or economic backgrounds.

This widespread gaming experience has big effects. Dr. Daphne Bavelier, a brain scientist, says, "The brain is very flexible, and playing video games changes the brain." These changes affect everything from how long people can pay attention to how they solve problems, potentially changing how a whole generation deals with life's challenges.

Different Types of Motivation

To understand how gaming culture affects us, we need to look at two types of motivation:

1. Intrinsic motivation: This comes from inside you. It's when you do something because you find it personally rewarding or enjoyable.

2. Extrinsic motivation: This comes from outside factors. It's when you do something to get a reward or avoid punishment.

Video games blur the lines between these types of motivation. The quick feedback and reward systems in games tap into our brain's pleasure centers. This might make it harder to feel satisfied with tasks that don't give instant rewards.

Dr. Richard Ryan, a psychologist who studies motivation, warns that "Relying too much on outside rewards can weaken inner motivation." This is important for personal growth, education, and community development, especially in African American communities where inner strength has been crucial for overcoming unfair barriers.

How Games Change Our Brains

Growing up with video games doesn't just change how we spend our free time – it actually rewires our brains. Research by Dr. Simone Kühn found that regular gamers had more gray matter in the hippocampus, a part of the brain linked to navigation and memory. While this might improve certain thinking skills, it also raises questions about how these brain changes affect other areas of life.

Author Lakeisha Vincent

BIOGRAPHY

Bullying and The Bystander Effect by Akiya Maston

Biography:

Akiya Maston earned her B.A. in Psychology, and an M.A. in Human Resources. After working in Corporate America for several years, she switched careers and found her calling as an educator. She taught high school for 10 years, then obtained her Educational Specialist degree and worked as an administrator for middle and elementary schools for 9 years. She is currently the principal at Pinewoods Elementary School in Estero, Florida.

During her 19 years working in education, she developed several educational resources, one is Music to Mastery, which helps elementary students learn Geography through 11 short songs and maps (www.MusicToMastery.com), and the other is, The Wonder Years of Middle School (www.WonderYearsBook.com).

Akiya Maston's Middle School Story:

During Akiya Maston's middle school years, she was never bullied but was a bystander to twin girls who were bullied nearly every day. She chose not to get involved for fear of being the new target. So, what did she do? Rationalized the bullying. "Well, if they dressed differently, acted differently, styled their hair differently then they wouldn't be getting picked on." This was 35 years ago and her own behavior, her lack of getting involved to help, still haunts Akiya to this day. Years ago, the age old mantra was "stick and stones may break my bones, but words will never harm me," We know now that words can be more hurtful, and the pain can also last longer with words. In the chapter, Bullying and Bystander Effect, Akiya shares the full story along with tips to help students and parents navigate scenarios such as these. Unlike, 1988, students not only face this type of torment but now there is also a social media component. So taunting lasts beyond the school walls.

1.) There will always be tough moral decisions facing you, and because you're young and living in the moment, you won't naturally think about how you might feel years later if you don't stand up for what is right now.

2.) If you hear something, see something, say something. I should have spoken up, given the fact that I witnessed the bullying nearly every day. I should have been an advocate for them, and maybe I should have been a friend or invited them to join my circle of friends. They could have been protected then, since bullies typically enjoy tormenting the lone student who has no support. It is important to share what you know with a parent/guardian, teacher, school counselor, or a dean.

3.) The negative experiences of the two girls could have extended to social media, which means, the torment might have continued even when they were not at school. Think of social media as if your family were standing right behind you when you write something unkind. Would you post if your grandmother were standing over your shoulder?

4.) You may find it challenging putting yourself in another person's shoes. I was so wrapped up in my own world that I did not fully understand what my two classmates must've gone through.

Let me also add that sometimes we may say or do things that hurt others without even knowing. I would recommend you to T.H.I.N.K. Before you post something online, ask yourself, "Is what I'm about to say: True? Helpful? Inspiring? Needed? Kind?"

5.) Bullies may treat other students negatively because of issues they are or have been going through in their own lives. People often treat other people based on how they feel on the inside. It's hard to give love and kindness if you don't have it for yourself. Hurting people hurt people. Sometimes, it takes just one friendly conversation to help another student's behavior change. If that doesn't work, or if you feel unsafe talking with that student, please share what you know with the proper authorities at your school.

6.) Social media was not around when I was growing up, but it is such a large part of young people's lives today. It is a way to stay connected. Just be sure to not share your passwords with any friends though. Did you know that if someone else goes into your social media account and says some unkind things, you may be held responsible for it, from the school's perspective? Also, once you post, it is out there forever, even after you delete it, post responsibly. Please keep all social media private so only your friends can view and comment. Having social media also means other people have access to you as well, which can include grownups with not the best intentions. I hope this goes without saying, but do not meet up with anyone whom you do not know. That could put you in very dangerous situations.

7.) Social media can also serve as a hotspot for comparison. You may feel that you are not as good-looking, athletic, popular, talented, or as smart as your peers. Remember, there's No One like you - all of us are born unique; however, many of us leave this life as "copies" – be unique, be you! The traits that make you feel "strange" are the gifts that make you special.

Success Tips for Parents/Guardians:

1.) I encourage you to have candid conversations with your children. Let them know of at least one bullying situation where you failed to stand up for a peer, or where you were bullied with nobody to stand up for you, or just maybe where you were the one standing up for what's right when someone else was bullied. Children are more likely to confide in you when they hear you say you experienced something similar to what they are going through today.

2.) Regarding social media, many platforms have a minimum age requirement of thirteen years old, which may be a good rule of thumb to follow in your household. For our amily, our children could not have social media accounts until high school, which eliminated middle school drama that typically stems from having it.

3.) If your child does have social media, it may be prudent to know their passwords or "follow" them so you can see all interactions. Now some children get crafty and have multiple accounts for the same social media application, and they will just give you a password for one of the "good, clean, innocent" accounts. It is important to have discussions with your child about trust and transparency.

Success Tips for Parents/Guardians:

4.) Keep in mind, with social media your children's world just got exponentially bigger than your world when you were a child. This new exposure can be a positive way to stay connected and to get to know other people; however, it can also be a catalyst for rumors being spread, and for cyberbullying. If you discover your child is the victim of cyberbullying, or if you were made aware of another student being the victim, it is important to contact the school immediate**ly.**

5.) I found out the hard way how some parents use their own social media accounts to vent about school issues before notifying the school. A family shared information on social media about a student bullying their daughter, and they criticized me, by name, as the Dean, for not helping their child. This venting resulted in other parents joining in complaining about my inaction and ineptitude. Interestingly, the venting parents never even brought the bullying issue to my attention or the school's attention before the online torment. The comments were extremely hurtful. Essentially, I was being cyberbullied for not protecting their bullied daughter.

6.) As parents, you are an example to your children of how to appreciate social media. Please never attack any school official via a rant on social media. Your kids are watching you, even if they pretend not to be. If there is an issue, please contact your child's school to speak with an administrator.

Author
Jennifer Johnson

To create your own, choose a topic that interests you. It can be anything from fashion and beauty to travel and the news. Once you have your overall theme, you can start brainstorming the content. Just starting? Design a memorable masthead with an equally memorable name. This goes on the cover and sets up the branding for your entire magazine. What style are you going for? Is it playful? Classic? Bold? A good masthead captures the essence of your magazine, so it needs to be flexible, meaningful, and consistent enough for future issues.

Next, think of a compelling feature for your cover story. This will be what draws your audience in. Make sure that you have accompanying visual content that immediately catches the eye. Include photos, illustrations, and other graphics to match. Appeal to your audience, choose the right fonts and images, and you'll have a magazine that people will remember for years to come.

Allyna Robinson Hughley

Award-Winning, Self-Published Author

Is family oriented and the 11th of 13 children. She has been married for 31 years and has 2 sons. She has a Bachelor of Science degree in Computer Science. Allyna served in the United States Army Reserve for 20 years and is now retired. She is currently employed with the Department of Defense as an IT Applications Manager where supervises a team which designs and maintains IT systems and supports military personnel and their families worldwide. Allyna believes in empowering and uplifting the young community. She hopes her creative writing will inspire children to laugh, dream, and be the best version of themselves.

Soft Cover, Grades: Pre-K thru 5th, Juvenile Fiction, Children's Social and Emotional Book, Family Book

Children's books teach readers a valuable lesson about appreciation. They provide social and emotional learning for our children. The books help readers to understand and manage emotions, make responsible decisions, maintain positive relationships, and show empathy towards others.

Contact: 757.717.3883
Website: Giftsaregivenwithlove.com
Instagram: @authorallynarhughley
Facebook: Author : Allyna R. Hughley

Grandma's Hands
by
Author Rolanda T. Pyle

ROLANDA PYLE

About the Book

Shonda is heartbroken. She just lost her mother, and now she has to move away to live with her grandmother, which means she will miss her friends and her favorite teacher. But her teacher shares something with her that helps Shonda. Today, millions of children are living with millions of grandparents and other relatives without their parents.

Link to purchase book - Grandma's Hands

https://www.authorhouse.com/en/bookstore/bookdetails/781856-grandmas-hands

123 Count
with Me
on Granddad's Farm
by Valerie D. Johnson • illustrated by Cee Biscoe

THANKS TO GOD FOR THIS VISION!

With heartfelt gratitude, I lift my voice in thanks to God for his divine vision that has brought such extraordinary authors and poets to my midst. Their brilliance and creativity have enriched my life and the lives of countless others. I am humbled by the gift of their presence and the beauty they bring to the literary world.

I give thanks to God for orchestrating the perfect alignment of circumstances that allowed me to connect with these wonderful souls.

It is a true testament to His divine plan and the power of his guiding hand. I am in awe of the ways in which God has brought us together, weaving a tapestry of talent, wisdom, and inspiration that continues to inspire us all.

In this moment of gratitude, I acknowledge God's grace and providence for granting me the opportunity to collaborate and learn from these gifted authors and poets.

May we continue to be guided by God's wisdom and love as we journey together, united by our shared passion for literature, the written and spoken word.

IN THIS EDITION...

ARTICLES &. MORE

BWA TEAM

P. Henson CEO, Founder
Felicia K - Administrative
Khoury S - Technical
Michelle H - Education
Taryn L - Operations
Valerie S - Editing
Taniesha C-P - Contributor
Talona C - Contributor